Making Things

Watch Me Plant a Garden

By Jack Otten

Welcome Books

Children's Press®
A Division of Scholastic Inc.
New York / Toronto / London / Auckland / Sydney
Mexico City / New Delhi / Hong Kong
Danbury, Connecticut

Photo Credits: Cover and all photos by Maura Boruchow
Contributing Editor: Jennifer Silate
Book Design: Michelle Innes

Library of Congress Cataloging-in-Publication Data

Otten, Jack.
    Watch me plant a garden / by Jack Otten.
        p. cm. — (Making Things)
    Includes index.
    Summary: A young girl demonstrates how to plant a flower garden.
      ISBN 0-516-23945-7 (lib. bdg.) — ISBN 0-516-23593-1 (pbk.)
        1. Flower gardening—Juvenile literature. [1. Flower gardening. 2. Gardening.] I. Title. II. Series.

SB406.5.O88 2002
635.9—dc21

                                                            2001037106

Contents

My name is Mark.

I am going to plant
a **garden**.

I will grow **green beans** in my garden.

Here are the green bean **seeds**.

I am going to plant the seeds in this box.

First, I pour the **soil** into the box.

Then, I make holes in the soil for the seeds.

I make each hole two **inches** apart.

I put one seed in each hole.

Next, I cover the seeds with soil.

I make sure that all of the seeds are covered.

Then, I pour water on the seeds.

The seeds need water to grow.

My garden is finished.

I put the box near the window.

The seeds also need lots of sunlight to grow.

Soon, I will have big green beans like these.

I cannot wait!

New Words

garden (**gard**-n) a place to grow plants

green beans (**green**-beenz) long pods with seeds inside that can be eaten

inches (**ihnch**-uhz) a unit of length; there are twelve inches in a foot

seeds (**seedz**) the part of a plant that grows into a new plant

soil (**soil**) dirt

To Find Out More

Books

Dig and Sow! How Do Plants Grow?
by Janice Lobb
Larousse Kingfisher Chambers

Plants and Flowers
by Sally Hewitt
Children's Press

Web Site

Kid's Valley Webgarden
http://www.raw-connections.com/garden/
This site tells you how to plan and plant a garden.
You can learn a lot about flowers and plants, too.

Index

About the Author

Jack Otten is an author and educator living in New York City.

Reading Consultants

Kris Flynn, Coordinator, Small School District Literacy, The San Diego County Office of Education

Shelly Forys, Certified Reading Recovery Specialist, W.J. Zahnow Elementary School, Waterloo, IL

Sue McAdams, Former President of the North Texas Reading Council of the IRA, and Early Literacy Consultant, Dallas, TX